A WAKE IN THE UNDERTOW

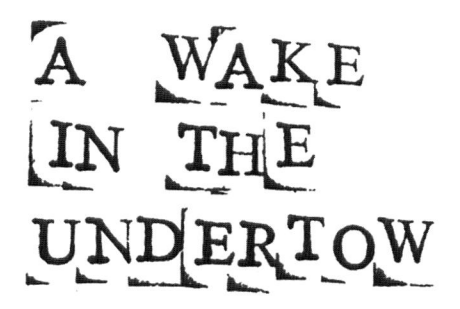

RUMBLE HOUSE POEMS

Rich Théroux & Jess Szabo

UpRoute
Books & Media

UpRoute
Books & Media

UpRoute Books and Media
An Imprint of Durvile Publications Ltd.
Calgary, Alberta, Canada

Copyright © 2017 by Rich Théroux and Jess Szabo

National Library of Canada
Cataloguing in Publications Data
Written and Illustrated by: Théroux, Rich and Szabo, Jess
A Wake in the Undertow: Rumble House Poems
Information on this title www.durvile.com and www.uproute.ca
ISBN 978-0-9952322-4-2
ISBN 978-1-988824-00-0 (ebook)

1. Poetry
First edition | First printing 2017 | Manufactured in Canada
"Have an idea" reprinted from *Stop Making Art and Die: Survival Activites for Artists*, published by UpRoute Books and Media.

Cover design and paintings by Rich Théroux
Inside pages design and typesetting by Jess Szabo
Post-production by Lorene Shyba

UpRoute Books and Media would like to acknowledge the support of the Alberta Government through the Alberta Media Fund.

All rights reserved.
Contact info@durvile.com for reprint permission or details.

Dedicated to Jess from Rich
and to Rich from Jess.

When masks
are forgotten
or at least
Comfortable
We relax a little
let guards down
stop wanting to be
perfect
or even (just) good
and out skids truth

a real brilliant truth
like a well-lit
hurricane

Art,
You are a goddamn mess
You're the kind of mess that makes clean people
Uncomfortable
Lucky for you
I am a nasty witch
Lucky for you I am at home in the dirt
My people came from the mud
We grow
We are fertile
We spread like ivy
We keep the clean people clean by contrast
they are sterile
we are doused in pigment
in the indigos and ceruleans
and all the luminous greys
not just the blacks and whites

Art,
You are beyond comprehension
You make the clear people sick

You make them question their
footing
lucky for you I dance on stardust
I don't need fenced boardwalks
To keep me on my path
I am lead by the light
We are lead by our hearts
heat sensors
pain sensors
we are lead to those in need

- - ->

Art,
You sure don't make it easy
to be truthful
to live wholeheartedly
to continually overflow and refill
Lucky for you we are not stones
Lucky for you
We are rivers
Each of us
And we'll keep picking up new
Gems
And passing them along
And spreading the love
And filling bellies
And quenching dry land
Lucky for us we have each other

Inherently I'm the bad dog
each valiant step an effort
I never sniff or wander
I don't eat the raw steak
I dont sniff the raw steak
Mangy, three-legged beast
I'll swat my own nose
All three paws on the path

no need to clip my nails

I wear them down too

More often
than I'd like to admit
my stretched ego puffs
against my rib cage envy rage and greed
D cell throat lozenges
float in back of my mouth
I'm supposed to be happy
I'm working on being
a real nice guy
but my heart
ill mannered
bad tempered
untamed dog-daily
I beat my own snout with
a rolled up paper to keep
from chewing the tassels off your Persian rug

Dear Malice. You make a tempting offer. But I think I'll stick it out with Hope for a while.
Love

At some age
As a right of passage
We were encouraged
To stuff off the imagination
Your Fluffy in the yard sale
    Like a lizard and its skin
    In place we nurtured
Vanity and greed
    How many windows
    How many cars
    How many bathrooms
    How much were your pants
Emblems even on your socks
My hat is off to you if
You weathered this storm
With daydreams intact
Your fortune is in your mind
If not your heart

Slow down
Everything you will
ever need is here
Breathe out until
the tank is empty
then slowly fill it
It's uncomfortable
to touch strangers
  with your hands
  with your mind
  with your heart
You are not alone
we are with you
whenever you feel ready

I hated
myself
as a kid
and I did
long enough
I'm still surprised
when I notice i don't
hate myself anymore
I remember thinking
on Valentine's day
who could ever
love me?
but I held on
and out came this
dream, and I carved
out a space to scream
I Love You I LOVE YOU
I LOVE YOU
and on
really good
days I
kinda
love
me
too

I'm told she's rather pretty
shadowed by the kindest
gentle heart

and how hand in hand
the magnitude of just
how bloody smart

or how off she'd
cut her arm
should you ask politely

cower against infectious
laughter as it bellows
off the moon

and how the light
will bounce on amber orbs
as bright as suns or moons

and if you still think
she's pretty
as pretty as can be

you still haven't seen
the pretty, the pretty that
I see

   in all her speckled
marvel and how she looks
      at me

I howl
I howl in this garish sunlight
Recoil and wail once more into
the unforgiving distances
banshee
  These are my lungs
  Filling with this acrid air
  I need you
Pump that morning dew
That sweet O2
  Straight to these rotting bags
    Hanging in this
    Ribbed cage
Designed to keep something contained
  Crack the gates wide
  Let this bird sing
  Let this bird scream

Magpie, you industrious little thief
you stole my bobble for
your arthritic woven shrine
I am told there are falcons
who never build their own
nests, they just wait for
you to get the itch to
move on your way
and when the city
cut down your tree
I thought this would be
the end for you and me
but you just keep plugging
you little turquoise bandit
you are the bastard of
your kin, and even my
blue-haired granny
keeps a loaded weapon
to greet you, what makes
you so loyal when all the others
fly away, and why does everyone
hate you? I really dig your song
I always will, and I always did

This poem is sloppy

you run out of your
favourite colours
taking down a show
is like taking a punch in the gut
painting can be
cripplingly lonely

it's hard to be happy
when your
friends leap forward ...
but we try

probably don't fit
your day job

there's always some
middle management
psychopath who torments
you for sport

you are a good target
and you never advanced at being nasty

some brushes are way better
than others
pencil sharpeners in your
pocket poke your thigh
scratch your phone

- - ->

14

you steal pens from
good people effortlessly
you speak with your heart
it's mostly broken all the
time and you rarely
know why

and all your heroes are dead and
they all died the same way

and it scares you
and that's not okay
There was one person
who really got you once and again
once there were
four people who really got you and
that was amazing terrifying

now there's more

maybe fifty?
it's hard to say
sometimes having to go
to the bathroom won't
pull you away

and you fight and you
scream for change
and things change
and you fight and you scream
again

By all means
break every law of art world
but make sure you
learn every law of art world
By all means

Our struggle is our capital
No one said it would be easy
you must stay feral as long
as you can
memorize the broken
moments
salivate, get up and shove against
something that leaves your
heart pumping
beat loud on that bloody drum

We cut our teeth
on rugged cliffs
on experience
we climbed
a human
rope ladder
made of arms
and thighs hands
and knotted toes
by sinew and heart
we beat together
all imaginable
odds and a
few new
ones
too
the business loan
wasn't money but
doled out in guts ...
a shitload of guts

Margaret
guide me through
This wilderness
The more you know
The farther you know
you have to go

Mother Mary
Lead my heart through
These tremulous tides
The clouds play games
And cover the stars
I try to steer this feeble vessel

Salome
Push this tired brain
Next step next step
Fling those veils

Whatever your privilege
Pass the surplus to the needs
of the village
Every advantage is a prison
Each dead end an excuse
To walk, to burn the fat
young man, little angel
Walk a little more
Collect only the sort
Of treasures you feed
Your mind
your compound interests
Will make you the kings
and queens
Of this earth

He is quiet
Alive
his eyes
are darts
striking everything
with dangerous
attention
it's murder to make
him speak
little me
he only smiles when
no one else is looking
little reckless soul
he tries on my shoes
laughs
at the holes
He knows I pace laps
beating fruitless tracks
for him alone to run unfettered.

Bound to agree with you

I'm high on exhaustion
Huffing life, fumes
twitching muscles
having a vascular
dance party in
my face to
celebrate
I think we found
our way home
not in the clear
still a little in the red
but definitely not
dead

May the dragons
snakes and sharks
come to know
your name
and step lightly
to stay out of your way

I'll find fifty street monsters
on my bike ride to school
Fifty more reasons to feel
like I don't want to go
Or I'll find fifty beautiful
angels dancing in the snow
on the lip of the bridge
over the frozen river
I'm only going to find what
I'm looking for
It's that easy
I'm only going to find what
I'm looking for.

The conduit

it passes through me
maybe you know it too
someone else's light
shining on the wall
or the canvas or
the page
or your
foot or knee, elbow
it passes right through
me and I read words from
another language or feel
the feel, the real god damn
feel of someone else's skin
it passes right through me
maybe it passes through
you too and I'm able to
do and see and be so
much more

My grandma told me
Heaven is going to be
Whatever I want it to be
This is what I want it to be
A red wood and velvet movie house
With brass knobs and greasy popcorn
And a 16mm film of my life
I can watch one run through
A short intermission to get
Liquorice (black) and glass of Tang
And one run of the film without me
Like an alternate version
Of my life when I wasn't born at all
And I could watch and see how
The world would have been
Without me
And that's all
Give my bones to the ground
And my mind to stardust
I'm wishing for that right now

Sometimes what we do
Can feel so incredibly
Beautiful that it just
stings and I have to sit
Down as if love
could be an allergic
Reaction heart attack

This poem is for
the nit picking ninnies
there just isn't time
to open your mind
to open the gap
wide enough
for your
enormous
head
if I had
to sink to your level
to hair pulling and cackles
or your ergonomic laptop
debate there wouldn't
be time to get
anything else done
I'm fine with your pebbles
it's the gloating I find
repugnant truth is
I teach junior high
and could out
juvenile you ...
any time I want
but I don't
mostly because
I know if you make me mad
enough
my sister will kick your ninny ass

By all accounts Henri Rousseau was considered a clown in his time.
Everything he did was wrong. He had to break in. Like a tank.
A bad ass gallery tank.

Life (love) on the run fill your
heart with love and hope and
RUN LIKE HELL

the nasty people
bogged down with greed
and envy and
bitterness
can never really breathe they
think they can
punish you
by choosing to
QUIT

Usually my tendons
Tie all the muscles to the bone
And veins and arteries
Loop my body red and blue
Tubes to keep my blood
Inside my skin and
my skin is a great
Big pink balloon bag
a wet rucksack
And gravity
(thank god)
Pins my feet
down
Just enough
That I don't fall away
Usually but
Today I'm using the
Brute force of my mind
To hold my shit together

Despite all odds
We carry on
Like the river

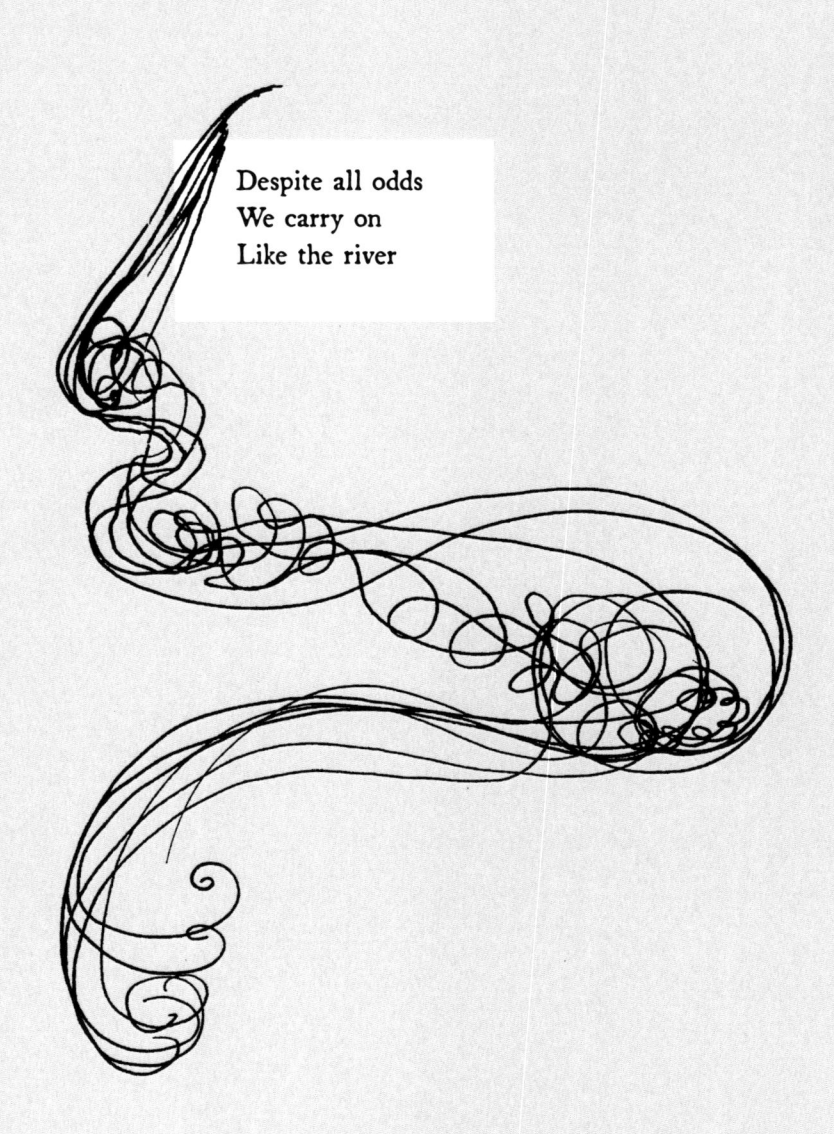

When you were a kid
Did you ever take a nap
In your dad's winter parka
Legs in the sleeves
And either your feet
Or shoulders were chilled
Because it didn't quite
Fit to cover you up?
Did you ever sleep in the back of
A station wagon on the way home
From Christmas at your Auntie's?
Do you remember how the blue
Street lights made your lips purple
Or that beam that would thread
Your car to the street lamp as
You drove swinging from one
Blue bulb to the next?
Were there whole days we didn't
Have to do anything at all
Filling time
Killing time
Waiting for the next one...
My whole body hurts
From bottom to trim
From worry about
Other people's worries
I think I might throw up
I wanna wrap up in a giant
Parka and take a snooze

Crippled by a desire
to make the world a better place
in a place driven
to expire

I promise myself
(the world)
I'll be ten men
today
It's lofty
arrogant
an earnest
attempt to be
ten men
Pulls me closer
to being one

If we scatter
While the world is
Collapsing we become
Fuel to the chaos
If we take shelter
We are ineffectual
Fight this storm
Fight this storm
A billion people holding hands
Close their eyes and make a
Wish
We pull the gangs and the unions
And the schools and the clubs
And the churches and the
Atheists and the masons
And the ... everyone
And together
Beat it all down
With a tsunami thought wave
Eyes closed together we imagine
Things back into order
We'll beat you with hope
We'll beat it with magic

For ages I watched the tigers in their cages
in I crept in the pitch of night
while the keepers slept
and unlocked
the gates
some ran
some stayed
i hoped some might love me
i knew some would hate me
the truly bitter lingered
and then they ate me.

Riverbed, we are
drawn finitely abreast
weaving the most simple
path back to the ocean
(to sea) (to see)

    Its cool
   come put your
    feet in the river
    I'm free
     drink me
    I'm beaten against
     the mountain rocks
   all damn day
    dance, fish, swim, camp
   I'm the river
  Come please play
   what's that?
YES
 you can
   be your own
    river too
  trace your way back
   to the source
   the dam you
    were building
   that's not the way
   trace your way to the
   source everyone knows a
    beaver is just a big ugly
    buck-toothed rat

Now I lay me down to sleep
I close my eyes'n
gently weep
  if I rise before I break
I'll do my best to
lift my weight
and carry forward
no more alone
friends and lover
and children born
and should promptly
opportunity
  obstruct my way
I'll abstain gently
no I won't rise
not until we all go
together
one more day
one more day
together

My little boy
flying
on his
little bike
  Reckless
  ran face first
into the corner of the
Table
    he cried a little
AND HE SCREAMED
WHEN I CLEANED
THE SCRAPE
and I put cream on his face
  and he promised
IT WILL GET BETTER
SOMEDAY
someday dad it
won't hurt anymore

In your heart
You know truth
It's evident in
Each breath
  The ache you
Inevitably feel
While you waiver
Listen to your
Damn heart

Little boy
little red wagon
to the rhino: you
can climb in my wagon
the rhino said thank you
and got in
it was heavy
little boy
little red wagon
to the hippo: you too
can climb in
the hippo said thank you
and got in
even more heavy
little boy
little red wagon
said to the billy goat:
there's room climb in
the billy goat thanked him
and did indeed
at the end of the road
the billy goat hippo rhino and
little boy with the wagon
came upon the man in
the suit
please sir would you help me pull?

not a chance, said the man
that's too bad, said the little boy,
sweating but still smiling

you'll want a ride with us soon.

Your fortune is love
and hope
and imagination
experiences
and you absolutely
can take it all with you

Remember that year when Prince and Bowie
and everyone went back up into the sun.
Remember we each stood up and asked,
"Am I giving it my all?" It seemed
ugly at the time but maybe that's when
things really began to change. when we started
living like them ...

They've been burning witches
and artists and scientists
since as far back
as we have had flames
and cord
 we manifest
 and we are dangerous

Things I've survived

The resource room

losing my REDLINE MX 3

calling my dad chief stupid face
that hockey team I lipped off
from Western
the guy at the LRT (knife)
art history
reading my first book
writing my first book
homelessness
parenting
homeless parenting
professional writing program
bathroom at Jambo Java
ripped my arm (bicep) off
Intuition (privacy)
Empathy (invasion)
that argument with Robin about
a Tiffany's bracelet
university
teaching
Gorilla House
public speaking
60 hour weeks
90 hour weeks
100 hour weeks
Once I survived a 125 hour week
divorce
getting my sunglasses stolen
these wakeful things
brought me this far
Here

Lists
and lists
hard work too
he builds
we clean
late nights
he builds
I clean
He writes
I stitch
We bike in the sunshine
work under moon
we watch a movie
we lay down and feel
the world spin around us
Inertia
We get up
world keeps spinning
hours keep spinning
so much to do
so little time
Art making
Art sharing
Heart-felt joy
Mountains
Wine
Tea
River
Love
A week off
It's never enough Time

I'd have dismantled myself
a thousand different ways
by now
if it wasn't for you
I like the way I look
in the tiny black reflections
of your big
cow eyes

Thank you for being
The glue I stitch my
Broken backbone
Thank you for being
The lens that bends
The light I need to see
Thank you for sleeping
In a sweat-soaked bed
my limbs don't know
Sleep they muster
In the night
The cluster knot and
Fight
Thank you for taking
That risk
To stand by me on
Whatever sinking tub
We've sailed
Thank you for
Holding my bones in
Place when the meat's
Been torn free
Just long enough
To heal
Or feel
Thank you for being
Able to see me in the dark
(My dark) or hearing me
Should the wind of nil
Rail. Awe. Thanks
For believing in me
So I won't matter
If I fail

Cause I've got you
And every step
we've taken this far

Thank you for forging
Your crazy ideas
Into reality
Thank you for taking
A shy, sad, disillusioned
25-year-old
And showing her all the
Opportunities
And joys life has to offer
Thank you for building a place
Out of grit and sweat
Hundred year old dust
And your own blood
Thank you for being so
Kind, understanding and
compassionate
That we feel safe
And braver
Just walking through the doors
Hundreds of kindred spirits
Have met under our roofs
We put our best selves out there
Vulnerably
And are caught by
A hundred gentle
Open palms
Thank you
The rain has washed the dust
Off the rumble wagon
This place has washed the dust
From existence
And it's shining and new

I need a new plan
Something better than
Becoming a mountain guerrilla
All the magic people I love are
Boiling in the Weltschmerz

I need a new plan
Packed in fat
Bound in love
The only weapons left are
minds and hearts

Oh man,
My heart hurts so much
And to tell you the truth
I really have no excuse

I just really love being alive sometimes
so much,

And I can feel the pulse of people in
me and
I take it all in

It swirls around inside me
Like a molotov cocktail
of disenchanted moments

I've never had an altruistic
Thought in my life
I help the people around me
trying to let the pain out
the window

Rain, sun, or tornado

I like the ostinato
I like the arabesque
I like the duplicity
and the ambiguity
I like the chirascuro
and I like you

So every day we live
we accumulate
not the meaning of life
but the business of cause

and effect
take a look forward
this day
what do you plan to
stick yourself to along the way
more stuff
will flatten your feet
more love more
experience will
lighten the load

Not just a canary
I'm a hard working
coal mine canary
who is listening to
my song?

Pinched fist and
open palm
Every single step
We push forward
To follow
Our hearts
It's not easy
as it looks

In that mad rush
to get from one place
to the next I stop
tip my face at
the sun and
let the love
sink in
without it i'm
a wet bag of meat

Hate is sticky
thoughtfulness takes effort
Simple ideas are easy to share
and love is complex
and we are doing a piss-poor job
of standing together
piss-poor
we are not winning
not right now
net even a little
not like this
and maybe
(if you are still listening)
you've grown tired
of my preaching
while we are flung into corners
it might be time to take cover

Sometimes you rattle the cage
To make change
Sometimes they box your nose
You stand or you drop
You keep shaking that box
Thinking you'll outlive them
with your anger
with your right
with your correctness
(you are not always right)
You know when NOT to fall
Ali had God on his side
(rumble young man rumble)
and they box your nose
AND YOU STUMBLE
but you don't give in
if you give up
IF YOUR GADDAMN MIND
GIVES UP before your body
GIVES IN
like a bad dog you better
not let them put you down
Rattle that cage son
Rumble Son Rumble

There's no Dracula
There's no goat foot devil
A personification of a thing with
a face and two tongues
I do believe in evil
I've felt it slither
And I've felt it
Piling up against me
There are shadows to avoid
Shadows to avoid

It's like this
We're going right
World's gone left
Maybe we're crazy
Maybe dumb
Not giving in
We'll beat down madness
We'll beat down gravity
with kindness

I won't quit
I won't fall
I won't slip away
I might not even die
I'm not to be bought
or sold or wooed I'm
the pebble in your
ever loving shoe
close your eyes
go into that deep
cozy sleep mmm
and when you wake
coffee will already be brewing
and you can
have a cup if you like
or grind your own
it won't change
a thing you'll
know I was up
all night waiting for you to wake
up too

It's been really amazing
This old bruiser
standing on the old bones
the muscles and the tendons
flayed by the storm
beaten past pulp
at any given moment
206 of us hold each one
of his bones in place so
like a giant skeletal puppet
He moves
He fights
and even when scavengers
snatch with greedy fingers
digits and vertabrae and
anything that shakes loose
he (we) somehow endure
Here comes the knock out punch
we all see it coming
it's a convergence
of catastrophe
here comes the end
here comes the knockout punch
no amount of resilience will
hold this old captain together
we give it our all
we close our eyes
out goes light

Love most
those things
you counted on
most
take for granted
those things
you counted on
most
Lose things you
took most for granted
regret loving those things
you counted on the
most
Repeat?

Art is tough
We endure
The flood was tough
We endure
The recession is tough
We endure
Getting rent gentrified was tough
but we endure
APATHY KILLS

Fringe
Just outside the line
Not enough for some mercy
Only just outside the line
Wasn't I born here too
Am I the same bone
And meat as you
Fringe almost
Always alone
In a crowd
You sad
Circus clown
Your painted face
Lies and your friends
The ape and the lion and
The strong man beaded
Tattooed stripper goat
We're all freaks too
Covered in fleas
One by one we
Scurry rodents
together we lit
The night the
Circus tent's
Ours alone.

How do villains sleep?
I try my best to do well
by the people around me
and I sweat laps
in my bedsheets
each night I wake up frozen
after I sweat (wet) the bed
for what deeds do the monsters
in my dreams want me to pay?
What does it take to clear my
plate so I could drift off for
rest just once I wake up
each day more exhausted
from the night than my day

go ahead and feel it deeply let it rip you
to shreds let karma seal your
body parts back in order
go ahead and feel it deeply

Aw. Shit.
When you
Live downtown
You know that shape
On the pavement
Sleep well
Jumper

It's pretty lovely
It's a pretty lovely life
And if I ever forget to
Notice there's Jess
Right next to me
Bubbling up in
Tears. "it's all
So beautiful."
She says. her
Cheeks beating Red

So. you can be edgy but
classy-edgy
you dig?

By giving
and not taking
We end up with more
than we can ever imagine
it starts with giving
a shit and then
not taking
any

Twirl till you're sick
my friend
if you can carry
on dizzy from the spin
yet carry forward
Dear drunken warrior
Should you ever need to throw
a punch. you do so
with the momentum
of the World

This is it
This is what we
Worked for
This is our life
So much more
Than we'd hoped
It's not as good
As it gets and it's
Not the worst
Those two honours
Come twice
In a lifetime
This is what we worked for
This is our life
Feel it
Feel it so hard
This is our life
It's pretty great
each second
Burning away.

You're there

Telling stories on
a microphone
Or a canvas
Being a beam of hope
When beams of hope are
few and far between

The fact that we're here at all
Making art together
In our little art hut
Is pretty damn
Lovely

Be strong
  be brave
    be gentle
    use your mind
    as your pry
don't wait for
middle
management
to support you
by their very nature
they will never stand
behind you
(on you, mind you)
but never behind you

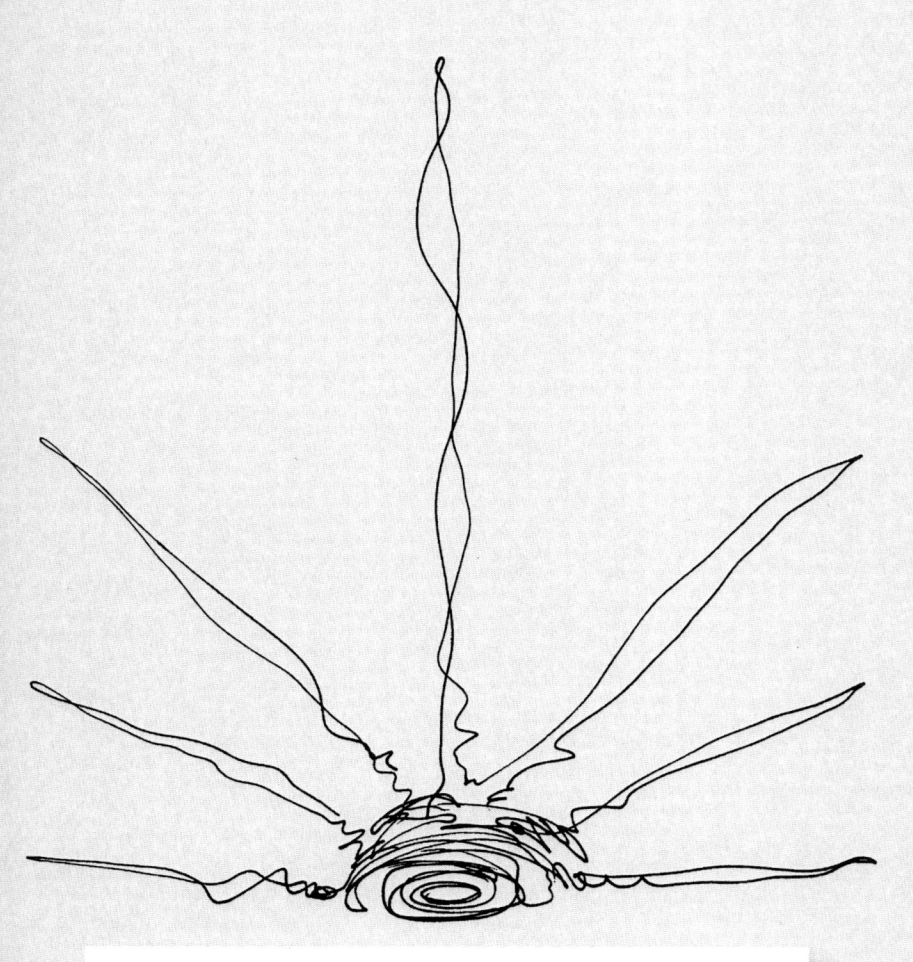

One sane voice
One rational thought
One compassionate heartfelt
Whisper is all you may need today
It wants to be so amazing, so let it

We don't need money
Just some moonlight
To shine down on us
While we dance

I've got at least 5 gifts
and at least 5 curses
and some days I'm cherished
and some days I'm worthless
and sometimes I lie
or write pretty
verses
you could say I am:
stupidly brave
sensitively weak
obviously strong

considerately shy
independently selfish
I'm made of 5 gifts
I'm made of 5 curses
5 plus 5 is still 5

Social climber
The top rung is
Packed with assholes
Work on your craft
Cherish your kin
Stop bending
and mounting
for the hierarchy
Lest you might arrive
The party is at the gateway
Where we dance limbs open
And the river meets the ocean
You know it's true
You feel it

Arms flung wide
Rib cages swung open
Hearts thunder
Wild vibrations
Where that river meets the ocean

Welcome home

And the fires sing
And the babies shriek with giddy
baby laughter
and no one tut tuts
and no one slows down to
correct or shame

While the drums are going
While the palms and fingers and limbs
are beating those skins
and taking it up

we dance three inches off the
Earth

invest in your mind
invest in the lives of
the people nearest to you
take care of the bohemians
it's okay to envy
their freedom
they live as a reminder of
when you were free
don't blame the stone wall
it's the edge we use to
sharpen our wits

I have so much more
than I ever wanted
got it by giving
everything I had
    away

When I paint myself
It's not because I'm pretty
It's how I try and shape
Reform myself into who
I need to be

When I paint Jess it's not because
She's pretty but rather the best way
to climb inside her skin

When I paint my children
I trap them in amber forever

My mom on this earth

Or the beat in my heart
Or the rhyme in my mind

To pull the colours out my
Fuggin eyes or how to
Spell the firealarm in
My ear that's a gong
to my own head

When I paint the sky
It's because I've leftover paint Mostly
the background is detritus

Jess is curled in a knot (like a cat)
she's cold she stretches one arm (now she's a snake)
I can't process her beauty
This is the kindest person I know
So lovely
I think back to when she was my best friend
I just really liked her
I just really, really liked her. so much
A canary (now bird) some poor fool would try to keep in a cage
I think about who I was last week, or last year or even before

I was a gorilla
How did she know she would love me?
I think she always knew
I had nothing but a working plan for a disaster
Wasn't she my best friend; unconditional love

- - ->

She unlocked (unblocked) everything good in me
She saw things I wouldn't dream of speaking
Wasn't I on a collision course with more disaster?
Like a mad man, wasn't I bent on destruction?
So when I walked forward, she came along by my side
(a mi lado)
Did she know she could love me? Unconditionally
Did I know? Or was it her own walk into disaster?
How could she have known, before she knew me?
before I knew me?
How did I get here? (hard work. insanely hard work)
Who am I? (she knows trust her)
How did I get this girl? (don't ask, let her sleep
when she wakes up kiss her) Kiss her nose when she wakes up
And be amazed, all day
All day

Sisyphus
How does it look
When you turn over?
What do you mean?
How does it look
When you restart
At the bottom?
I'm sorry?
When you reach the peak
And have to start over?
How does it look to...
How does what look?
... to start over
What?
... what are you doing there
I'm pushing this rock
Of course I am
... where are you going
To the top
Of course I am
... how long until you get there
I don't know
It's been taking a while
Why so long?
I keep having to start over
Oh, and what does that look
like?
...
It looks like morning

Life is pretty real on our block
I know you couldn't
wait to be on your way
I don't blame you for moving on
I'm gonna sit
I'm gonna stay
don't let yourself resent me
because I remember
where you came from
Life is pretty real here

Bob Dylan lay
Down on the couch
And put his head
Between two pillows

While the children
Played his reconds
Getting fired up about
Freedom

The grown-ups
Looked away

Fuck you Bob Dylan

Mr. Theroux did Jesus walk on water?
Take off your shoes
Take off your socks
Wiggle your toes...
 Look at those toes!
 You need a miracle?
 You have toes!
Mr. Theroux
Why is the sky blue?
 Easy! Orange is lazy, red is a show off
Blue never gives up!
Mr. Theroux what is the meaning of life?
Are you kidding?
 Are you *ucking kidding me?
The meaning of life is so easy!
This moment!
This moment is the meaning of life!
You are alive and you have this moment!
You have this moment and if this is the only
moment you ever get it's pretty
Wonderful
But you've got so many
Many many more
Don't you ever condescend
To ever take it for granted
You have THIS MOMENT
Don't YOU dare (ever)
Take it for granted.

I've got a poem
Inside me this morning
I can't get it out
It's lodged in my throat
Down near my heart
I've got the best
Warmest
Most dear
poem inside
Me and i must have
Meant to save the
muther....... world
With it
But I couldn't pull it out
And it's tearing me
Apart

We're made of ancient suns
fuelled by the sky fire of sol
we're meant to burn
Burn mother burn

Art and pain
Work fine
But there is
Still love and
Soul and Beauty
We needn't seek out
The strife to create
Paint with your
Heart it's okay to be
Happy you can still
Paint for joy and Love

I'm going to write a poem
About not thinking about
Politics
And the girl in the room
Who keeps all my hope
And about being born with
Luck in my jeans (genes)
And a back I never broke
And friends who'd
Walk through the night
Looking for me
If I were lost even
In the darkest places
And how in the summertime
Walking around in the dark
In shorts and a plain white T
Waiting for a thunderstorm
Drinking a slurpy
With sun Burnt skin
Sun burnt skin in the dark cool
Night and the moon licked wind
And my kids who keep growing
More interesting than me
And those strong brave trees
That last 500 years
And like Gandhi said
Eventually they fall
And all will be good
Or nothing at all

How do How do I
How do I look my
Son in the eye and say
The benchmark for gentlemanly
behaviour has been removed
just flat out obliterated
be better than your
dad. be better
than your
teacher
and for ---
sake be better
than the president
of the united states

Flow over
Be a river son
The mountains are
Tall and you can flow
All year, all day, all night
Without fear of running dry
Be a river son and overflow
With love for your brothers
And sisters hope and love
There's no bank for it
There's no safe
Be unsafe
Flow across
The whole world
Splash the cities with
Your indiscriminate love
Splash the people and
Their cars and wash
Their feet in your
wake
Flush the sewers
Be Unstoppable
Be Fearless
Be the river true

Concentration/Tension
Levels of Intensity
Awareness of medium and tools
inventiveness
Awareness of Boundaries (rocking the boat)
Compositional Risk Taking
Skillfulness with light
Skillfulness with gravity
Knowledge/ Context place and time
A sense of blood, skin, atmosphere
Movement and/or Stillness
Historical Reference and/or Rebellion

Allegory, Narrative, Cleverness

Depth, Mark making
Earnestness
Emotive Response

Dear God
Make my words
Hard like atom bombs

Let me break the shells
Of those bigot minds who've

Set themselves to harm your
Muslim children or
That would close doors
On your daughters
That would feed the rich
And eat the poor
Let my hands have the
Strength to hold the
Largest hammer
And bash down
Prison
Walls
Borders
Your beautiful black
And brown and red
or navy children
all colours of the rainbow
There is dinner for everyone
on this green earth
If we can only make our
Words hard enough
To break the walls
Of stupidity
To cut scar and
Heal from scratch

I'm not growing potatoes today
And I won't be butchering a pig
but I'm still going to want to eat
so I guess rather than feeling
so damn sorry for myself
I better get out of bed
and find a way to
keep the people
in this village
this earth
glad that
I am part
of this life
and some forgiveness
for the people who can not see
past wanting more (for less)
and just be glad I can
stand still and face
one more day
we all trudge
past the same
sunny meadows
we all want to lay
down in the grass
and later we will all
want to eat a potato
we all drink from wells
we did not dig

I get why people want to
play up the suffering
art making isn't a chore
or punishment
it's the only thing
that kept me
from a life of crime
and or madness

When I do it I feel good
When I feel bad
I can make myself well
if I just take some time
to work

When I don't I feel the
Whole (hole) inside me
Grows bigger

It's that hole that won't be
filled

And then sometimes
people pay me

and that's nice too

I used to have super hearing
Before I broke my ear
Really super hearing
I used to like my soft brown hair
I used to be so strong
and fit
and fat free
I used to stay up
All night eating my loneliness
I felt no hope
And so
so
so alone
I used to feel
So purposeless
(and so so alone)
and useless
I remember
Looking at
The sky
Wishing so
Hard for someone

– – –>

Just like you
It seemed
Impossible
So hopeless
So impossible
And so so hopeless

And so
Can you imagine
What it was like
To come unstuck
To come unstuck from
The pain and
Isolation

And see so many people
Stuck in the sand

With two perfectly
Good ears

And they won't hear me

"You are not alone"
You are not alone

This is my promise
I'll stand
And you might take a
Swing
And you might not miss
But I'll stand
And you might knock
Me down with a truck
But I'll get up and stand
And you might kill me
But I have a soul
And I'll stand
Right here
By you
Until you are ready
I'll stand by you
Infinitely as long
As you need
I'll stand
Here
This is my word

We come from proud people
Our people put mankind on
The moon
And our people built the sphinx
and blew off it's fuggin nose
our people built Auschwitz
and dismantled it
built up apartheid
and tore it down
Our people made donald trump
the leader of the free people
of the world
Our people recorded Mood Indigo
Our people are we, they, and you
We are one
Oh the things we have done
Oh the things we will do
He, she, they, we,
and you

Have an idea.
It's energy
It's free
Let it grow. Fester.
Don't sit, it seeps out
and will impregnate someone else.
Draw. Write. Shape. Sculpt.
Shove or let go.
Shove.
Find a space. Big. Bright and dirty
If it's dirty and no one would set
foot inside, it's for you.
If it's bright
Pull down walls
The ragged ones in the basement
the fence outside
the matter between the homeless
and the owners
the walls suffocate communities
Gravity economics and science
pull down the walls that
keep people out and make it free
it will take time for the shock to
wear off. Hit 'em hard when they're dizzy

- - ->

Clean up. Scrub paint.
there's 13 drug needles in the parking lot.
That's your security deposit.
Dumpster after dumpster.
Hug. Kiss. Whisper.
It's yours as long as you pinch a fist.
Fight. Boy you'll paint with one hand
and ball the other.
Crazy people need love too.
sometimes they get rough.
be rough boy, be rough and gentle
don't get hurt
Keep the little ones safe
pretty girls and rich people and that
guy with no pants
and the gaping crowd
It's scary throwing out those needles.
Be scary boy. This old building
is coming down so you can rent it.
Keep it clean. Not too clean mind you.
Keep it safe.
Beautiful is on the inside.
Take a risk boy. Have me.
I'm yours.

There've been days
There've been days I didn't
Think I'd take
One more step
Days I wouldn't sleep
One. two three. 72 hours
straight
There were days I didn't eat
Nor did I want to
Nor did I hope
There have been days
I wouldn't believe
Couldn't believe I'd stomach
To think of
I wince and turn my face
When I remember
And there were days like this
So good
So pure
So lucky
Did the universes shape me
for acceptance
Did I need my ass kicked
To really see
I'll never take another
goddamn minute for granted
(grated)
Grit my teeth days reborn
nothing will ever take this
Day (today) from me

Let us tell you something
So far we've been gently nudging
For an effect
But starting right now
We're going to hammer for radical
Change
Brace yourself

ROBIN SPARKES
HARPER LEE
GERTRUDE STEIN
BLONDIE
JUDY CHICAGO
NINA SIMONE
MOM
GEORGIA O'KEEFFE
JENNY HOLZER
KIM DEAL
JONI MITCHELL
SE HINTON
BUFFY
QUEEN LATIFAH
AUDRY HEP BURN
SAINTE MARIE
MARY MAGDAL
MC CARTNEY
FRIDA
PATTI SMITH
HOLLY WOODLAWN

GENE RODDENBERRY
MAURICE SENDAK
JIM HENSON
ROD SERLING
BUDDY RICH
MILES DAVIS
LEONARD NIMOY
Shel Silverstine
STEVE MCQUEEN
GEORGE LUCAS
PAUL McCARTNEY
MUHAMMAD ALI
NELSON MANDELA